Myths Don't Frighten Me

Written by Jonny Walker

Illustrated by Jim Crawley

Collins

Before I knew my special identity, my sister Summer and I were typical kids.

Summer always knew our precious secret, but decided not to share it until I needed to know.

There were early glimpses of my greatness.
Neighbours cheered when I sang in the shower.

School teachers mentioned that I had a strange glow.
I thought it was just an unusual compliment.

At last, my obsession with Greek myths caught Summer's attention. When I read old myths, they felt more like memories than stories.

6

"Hey, Summer," I asked, "how can this collection of ancient tales feel ... so real?"

Her expression was strange. "Kam ... I cannot shield you from the mythical world any longer."

"Myths don't frighten me," I said.

"They should. They are our family history," she replied. Then came the bombshell. "We are not Kam and Summer. I'm Artemis and you are Apollo."

Our father erased your memories with a mystical potion," she explained. "He hid us here in Doncaster. We need to seem like mortals to complete our mission."

"What mission?" I asked.

"There's a prophecy that atrocious monsters from our time will emerge here tonight. Do you remember Python?"

Visions from the past roared suddenly into my mind. I remembered Python. I remembered everything from before.

"Sprint to town quickly. Defeat Python before it destroys Doncaster. The mortals must not know that we and our enemies still exist," Summer said.

"But ... how can I bludgeon a beast with no weapons?" I asked.

"Check this out!" said Summer. "Father said you'd know what to do." She handed me a silver bow and four golden arrows. "Go now, Kam! Slay the beast before the town awakens!"

When I arrived, Python's huge shape had plunged the streets into sheer darkness.

The shopping centre was a scene of destruction. Python thrashed and roared. Three cleaners attempted to hide behind their mops. I cracked my knuckles and shouted, "Python!"

It surged up to me. The cleaners looked dumbfounded as I peered courageously into the serpent's eyes.

Python lunged and I dodged its gnashing jaws.
Aiming straight between its eyes, I fired
a golden arrow.

It struck with perfect precision. Python fell. The weight of it shattered the windows. I knelt breathlessly.

Amidst the destruction, Python melted to dust.
Then, the cleaners started to sweep up the ashes.

"Yuck! Where did this mess come from?" the oldest
cleaner whinged.

It was mind-boggling! They were acting like nothing
had happened!

Then I saw Summer holding an open jar. She was wafting a strange mist over the cleaners.

"Vapours from the River of Forgetfulness," she whispered.

"You could have helped before!" I said.

"Didn't want to interfere! It's *your* ancient grudge. I'll help on the next missions."

"More missions?" I said, uncertainly.

"Yes! We must protect Manchester from harpies! Let's go, Apollo!"

Apollo

Son of the Skyfather

God of Light

Plays a precious instrument

Artemis

Daughter of the Skyfather

Goddess of Hunting

Protects a special deer

25

Ancient prophecy

Oracles gave advice and made predictions. There was an important oracle at Delphi, ancient Greece.

Some Greek myths mention that Apollo first battled Python there.

Apollo versus Python

The story of Apollo's mission has been shared for thousands of years. Some ancient writers state that Apollo was just a baby when he killed Python!

This myth represents the battle between good and bad.

🐾 Review: After reading 🐾

Use your assessment from hearing the children read to choose any GPCs, words or tricky words that need additional practice.

Read 1: Decoding

- Can the children identify the different spellings of the /or/ and /j/ sounds after reading these words?

caught	roared	four	before
stories	strange	bludgeon	jaws

- Bonus content: Ask the children to read pages 24 and 25. Ask them to find the spellings of the following sounds: /i/ and /sh/, /or/ and /ear/.

Read 2: Prosody

- Turn to pages 16 and 17, and model using a storyteller voice to create drama and excitement. Discuss how you are speaking in character, too, because this is Kam's description (and perhaps he wants the reader to be impressed).
- Discuss the words you chose to emphasise and how you varied your volume, pace and tone. Encourage the children to take turns to read the pages out loud.
- Bonus content: Ask children to read pages 26 to 29 as if they are a broadcaster on a programme about ancient myths. Encourage them to think about which words they should emphasise to make the meaning clear, and to hold the listeners' attention.

Read 3: Comprehension

- Ask: What monsters in myths do you know about that might scare some people? Why might they be scary?
- Discuss the title and who **Me** is. (*Kam*) Ask: Do you think he was scared at any point in the story, or was he just pretending not to be scared? Encourage the children to back up their views by referring to the text.
- Point to the word **bombshell** on page 9. Ask: What does this mean? Explain the idiom, "drop a bombshell", a metaphor for giving shocking news. Ask the children to check this meaning makes sense in the context of the story.
- Ask the children to retell the story using the illustrations on pages 30 and 31 as prompts.